AF424371

Fighting Words

Jasmine Fox

Fighting Words © 2023 Jasmine Fox

All rights reserved.

No part of this publication may be reproduced, stored in a retrieval system, or transmitted, in any form or by any means, electronic, mechanical, photocopying, recording or otherwise, without the prior written permission of the presenters.

Jasmine Fox asserts the moral right to be identified as author of this work.

Presentation by *BookLeaf Publishing*

Web: www.bookleafpub.com

E-mail: info@bookleafpub.com

ISBN: 9789358319927

First edition 2023

Word Birds

Grant to yourself the gift of sight,
The power to feel a million Springs.
Let all your fledgling words take flight.

Thrust forth your pen with all its might,
Be as the blackbird when it sings.
Grant to yourself the gift of sight.

Each word must be a soaring Kite,
An Eagle, your untamed Starlings,
Let all your fledgling words take flight.

Break off the shell to reach new heights,
Each promise needs the strongest wings.
Grant to yourself the gift of sight,
Let all your fledgling words take flight.

On Tap

On tap; tap out
Switch off; redoubt
Touch grass; set about
Buckle in; catch clout.

Get good; good game
Dig deep; reclaim
Pull rank; dead name
Shake down; body shame.

Punch line; line toe
Lock down; re-echo
Brush aside; onward show
By the book; ungrow.

Vox Lyrical

Sometimes I feel
Set adrift on
Seven seas of
Suffocating
Nothing
Empty
Shivering inside

I feel like I
Don't belong here

Might as well
Learn to fly
To get away
Way up high

A Bit of Clutter

"It's a bit cluttered"
Life
Living
Lifetimes
Sieving

Wading
Wasting
Yearning
Chasing

Memories
Rare gems
Must haves
Never ends

Treasured junk
Worthless gold
New obsessions
Passions old

Battlements
Fortress
Barricade
Buttress

Mine
Me
Touch
See
More than stuff
Security

Just a Jar

My spoons for a jar.
Junk apparently,
But now exactly
The thing I need.

Just a jar
To make you better,
To hurry the pain away.

A jar
For my feelings
To save them;
To keep them
From hurting.

A jar
For wishes;
happiness, comfort,
Confidence, care,
To remind you you're wanted
When I can't be there.

A jar.
A stronghold. A fortress.
A keep.

Cylindrical armour.
To protect.
Keep it safe.

Lost: The Words (Part 1)

Where were you when
I couldn't breath
Going home again?
The unquiet road
A spear through my soul,
A sliver impaled
Behind me
Forever.
New dawn scorches my
Bone-dry eyes,
Wraith-like
A fare balloon
Harries the skies.
Windmills,
Hypnotic,
An angel's last stay:
Forever lost,
Walking away.

Dawn Raid

Thank you for understanding
We don't want to live this way,
The malodorous air, off-colour walls,
The grubby window bay.
The Everest of washing up,
That's hi-jacked half the bath,
The laundry-covered kitchen floor,
The takeout aftermath.
We see the mess. We know the rules.
We hear you warning "Danger".
You come, dissect with your five-minute eye,
But to our world, you're still a stranger.
Grasp that we are but one person,
Two halfs of a hardly whole.
A meld of adequacies ill-equipped
To pay the world its toll.
Impounded in our open cage,
Our gaolers, Body and Soul.
Help never comes, else goes too soon,
And seldom stays for pleasure.
How would you spend a fractured life,
In endless burnout or in leisure?
Incrementally, we do our best,
But band-aids won't mend bones,
And snowballs rolling down a hill

Will gather moss and stones.
Of course, it hurts, we're not abstruse,
When inspectors come to judge.
We've admonished our respective ails,
They don't seem inclined to budge.
So unless you've come with answers
Or to lend an earnest pair,
It's time to go, your 'little chat' has left me
Wiped out in my chair.

Lost: The Words (Part 2)

What will I be
When the rhythm won't play,
When the page glares back,
The ideas don't stay.
When the nib's bone dry,
The keyboard shot,
When the drive stops booting,
When the memory's rot.
What is a poet,
Without words,
What?

Rage

I'm so angry,
But not at you.
Don't ask me why,
I've not a clue.

I want to lash out,
To kick down a door.
Have an urge to shout,
To pound at the floor.

Run now, my Darling,
Flee from my wrath.
It's not meant for you,
Just don't cross my path.

Brick through that window,
Then flail with my fist.
Smash up that stereo,
What's next on my list?

I really don't know,
Why I feel like this.
Would you please just go,
I'm scared I won't miss.

Here Be Dragons

Land of Hills, Land of Song,
Land where a stranger may belong.
Land of Mountains, Land of Old,
Land of Myths and Legends told.
Land of Magic, Land of Streams,
Land of long forgotten Dreams.

The Dragon sleeps,
Beneath a lake,
The Bell will toll,
And Justice wake.

Land of Distaste, Land of Naught,
Impostors where there Dragons ought.
Land of Bigotry, neighbour scorned.
Noble lost, no Valour mourned.
Land Not My Fathers, but Land of My Youth,
Rise again, proclaim the Truth,
That Honour which for once you stood,
Shall stir again, and Wrong come Good.

Aftermath

Rumours.
Mean nothing to me.
Usually.
"I don't know how true it is."
That's what she said.
But still.
I'm on edge.
Someone told her.
It was someone he works with.
They had dinner with the person.
Who knew.
Ridiculous.
But it could still be true.
Oh, they may laugh it off.
And smile.
They're just in denial.
They're thinking about it.
Like me.
They'd be inhuman.
Not to be.
So here I sit.
Worrying.
Wondering.
Writing away.
Just in case.

It could turn out to be true,
Then now someone knows.
I knew.

Deluge

Maelstrom
Whirling, swirling, hurling, unfurling
Cluster bomb
Atomise, agonise, paralyse, cannibalise
Tsunami tide
Infuriate, exacerbate, annihilate, hyperventilate
Bio genocide,
Prophecy procured, vitriol inured, scrape your
gravestone word, survival unassured

Castellation

Who are you to
Look down on me?
We are not the same.
Our childhoods weren't equal.
There was us and you,
The Little General, who
Always got the lions' portion;
Us menials got half to share
If we were lucky.
No scrutiny besieged your cloisters,
No extorting daggers carved your back.
Never endured threats of exile,
Nor intimation that you were
A blood begotten hindrance.
Think of that existence,
The putrid stench of your own fear,
Terrified to step out of line, voice a thought,
Perpetually defending a waning spit of clay.
The constant shove and jerk of
Being made to compete for
Scraps of conditional affection.
Imagine growing up feeling
That all the subservience in the world would
Only ever win you third place.
It took an age for me to forgive myself

For my part in that pointless war.
We're allied now,
And the tyranny of You
Is a hobbled mouse trying to
Scale the ramparts of our
Vindicated empowerment.

Now You Don't

The many-headed mask you wore,
A herculean weight lashed around your neck.
We mourn those faces,
The impact they were.
Our lives, never really touched,
A one-way mirror;
Every move, performance,
Question, response,
Analysed, scrutinised.
As if any one of us could
Tear down the veil,
Turn back the clock,
Give you back to yourself,
The who before all the other lives
You gave to us.
Each voice completely yours,
And uniquely their own,
Louder than that seed of soul,
That screamed and flailed,
Yearned and travailed,
To be greater than
Your patchwork persona,
To hoist your coat, and walk tall
Beneath it.

Now and Then

Now and then I think of
How my life used to be.
Things that brought me Joy,
That I can no longer do.
Despair for things I'll never
Be well enough to enjoy.
Dreams dissolved like candy floss
In hot water.

Blazing leaves crunching
Under my boots,
Mottled light blinding through
The green canopy of
An impromptu nature walk.
No snowball fights,
Running and ducking,
Squealing laughter,
Loving each moment.
Tides so cold, and sand so warm,
Feet prickle in delighted confusion.

How can I compete with her?
See how vibrant she was,
The freedom she danced in?
I think, "I'll go mad".

Sometimes, I mourn the seaweed
Caught around a wheel spoke,
Dragged along;
A loved one determined
We'll reach the water mark,
Feel the salty spray
On my cheek.
Then, I remember to live
The loves I have, and
Try to forget that one day,
They might be gone too.

<<DATA: PROCESSING ERROR>>

Error.
Error.
Syntax incorrect.
Please rephrase: Loss of data imminent.

Scrub surface cache.
Multiple viruses detected.
Delete all logs, pending reset.
Incomplete database; defrag required.

Situation unrestrainable,
Current parameters unsustainable.
Hard drive reboot unattainable.
Memory kernels corrupted.

Core overload.
Critical temperatures exceeded.
System failure inevitable.
Destruct sequence commencing.

In 5.
4.
3…

Abort?
C:\LOAD Earth.2?

Self-Sabotage Squad

A gang of degenerates
live in my head.
They like to give me grief.
They chant things at me,
Dawn 'til dusk,
To erode my self-belief.
There's Inner Critic,
Fear Itself,
And ImpoSyn, the chief.

Inner Crit's
The judgemental sort,
Who points out all my defects.
He riles up
Ms. Perfectionist,
Blockading all my projects.

Fear Itself's
A tricky one;
Her opponent undecided.
Does Fame or Flop
frighten her most?
All confidence, subsided.

Imposter Syndrome,

a beastly troll
Who'll throw his weight about.
No matter where
I strive to fit,
He'd have them turf me out.

More than these three
Plague my brain;
A legion parasite.
Their grotesque damnation
Imprisons Creation,
So snatch up your sword and Write!

The Gamble

Villainy disgraced
Stop teasing me
Consequences faced
Stop teasing me
Sentencing fast-paced
Stop teasing me
Just an aftertaste
Stop teasing me

Uncontestable raid
I'll not hold my breath
Jury won't be swayed
I'll not hold my breath
Debts be fully paid
I'll not hold my breath
Flung in the stockade
I'll not hold my breath

Toxicity disperse
Don't count unhatched eggs
Atrocities reverse
Don't count unhatched eggs
Equality converse
Don't count unhatched eggs
United Universe
Don't count unhatched eggs

Still Life

Window, needs cleaning,
Curtains, always drawn.
Cat always lounging on the sill
Backend looking worn.

This isn't public access
You are not Nancy Drew.
My cat is well looked after,
Nothing to do with you.

Yes, she has a collar,
As her fur she likes to chew,
Food and water, veterinary care,
Whatever I can do.

Don't assume you know the novel,
By reading just the blurb,
And make no judgements on a life,
From outside on the curb.

TFW

That feeling when
You find yourself missing
The days of four
Channels on the telly.
Of turning off Newsround
Because there was
Something better
On the other side.
Of not being bombarded by
Dozens of screens a day,
Spewing reems of putrid
Human atrocity
Into your ears, eyes, brain.
When soap operas were
The only narrative the
Public consciousness
Rallied around,
United for, divided against,
Speculated about.
When truth was less
Deranged than fiction,
And we weren't addicted to
Instant consternation.

Up The Antics

Play the fool for peace;
Weirdos against aggression.
Random acts of kindness
Ignite a reconnection.
A funny sign, a daft outfit,
Spark a conversation.
Wave at the train, make someone smile,
A win-win wish projection.
Press the buttons, sing in streets,
Start a hat collection.
Leave cheerful notes for folks to find,
Feel fulfilled by reflection.
Be mad for good, out there for better,
A human hope injection.

www.ingramcontent.com/pod-product-compliance
Lightning Source LLC
Chambersburg PA
CBHW060232170726
48004CB00004BA/1515